Chashm- I- Dil
"The Heart's Eyes"

A Collection of Poems on Love, Life and God.

Sakina Abbas Ambawala

BookLeaf Publishing
India | USA | UK

Made with ❤ on the BookLeaf Publishing Platform
www.bookleafpub.in
www.bookleafpub.com

Dedication

For younger me,
Here's to living your dreams.
& to every voice that wants to be heard.

Preface

Chasm -I- Dil "The Heart's Eye's" a collection of poetry on Love, God & Life. Growing up I always questioned the world and its systems around me, Often praised by adults for being a logical thinker it would mark the beginning of a lifelong quest to finding meanings, patterns and sense into some important questions like "Is God real?" "What does it mean to Love?" and "Why do I exist?" the answers to these would then fall into my life as lessons and challenges that would refine my character as an Individual. This deep journey of soul searching would give birth to the existence of my own poetry book.

Acknowledgements

I would like to thank :

Allah Almighty for guiding me in life,

Friends who have always supported me in all my endeavors

Family that has been my source of strength

And every person that believed in my poems more than I did.

The Marigold flower

Saffron and Green
The marigold flower has both,
The green stem without which the flower doesn't sprout
The delicate petals of marigold with which the stem has
rays of suns on it's head.
But, can one exist without the other?
Will the green perish without its lover?
Does the flower not yearn for its support?
So how will you buy a marigold flower and separate it
both?
How do you remove the heart of the country and not see
how it suffers?
Why don't you see?

Half a heart

Half a heart,
Being born with half a heart
Is indeed a misfortune
You keep looking for the missing part
But is nowhere to be seen.
You think you finally found it
But it just doesn't fit.

You search for it relentlessly
But it never crosses paths with you,
You find this as God's most cruel test
Because how unfair is half a heart.

Everyday, every minute
Your pain deepens,
You share your dreams and hopes with another
To find your missing heart
But yet the stars never align.

You wonder,
You ponder,
Maybe this is not a test
Maybe there is something more to this
God, music, movies, poems

You try to fill the void
Until,
Roll out the prayer mat,
Standing in the direction of the *kaaba
Hands raising in prayer
And in the name of God
You finally find half of your heart.

(*Kaaba = The Kaaba is the qibla, or direction of prayer for the Muslim community)

Midnight romance

Midnight Romance

In the late night at 1 or 2
There is a romance that brews,

One which tells the stories of my dreams
Where I still look at the moon and the streams.

In the blankets of stars I hide my tears
The sadness that's etched away is near
I know that this happens often, yet I am unclear
If tomorrow will be a bright day or will I still be here?

There I hear, the footsteps to my destiny
I can see some path but not a direction maybe
Just what does life hold for us all?
Who are we? Before we were born?

Hide ourselves in the shadows
And the light keeps pouring in
I hold myself through it
But now I'm done with it.

Orange and white stripes

The tiger,
Within me and
Without me are often so different
The struggle to capture its glistening eyes
The dark hours of the forest and the slow paced walk of
its soft paws
So divine & fierce
I wonder does the tiger ever think, if its weak?
If it ever thinks of being more soft?
Does it pounce on everything?
Or waits for the right moment.
Isn't what we fear the most
We love the most as well?
My lover, and their love.
The Tiger and The Tigress
A beautiful world.
Being a Tiger is a choice
I will make it today.

Indian summer sadness

Mangoes
Slice open the yellow golden fruit
Drips it's sugary sweet goodness
Hold it tight, hold it right

Cut four pieces
Small cubes, so bite size
Bite right into it
Ouch, stings like the bees now

"What's wrong?"
"It's gone bad I think"
"But they look so tempting and sweet"
Not everything is all it seems.

Don't be sad, just a fruit.
Happens often to you
Let it be,
Don't cry, it'll be okay soon.

Childhood love

We were little,
Little hands, eyes and dreams
I your friend
And you my love.
The little fire in my heart
Grew with each passing year
A spark to a sun
And then came the crescendo
Crashing of two waves
The ignition of your flame
The beginning of us'
But the flame was too big,
Like I would remember
The collapse was like a star
A nebula
Ashes everywhere
A broken heart.
We were little,
Little hands, eyes and dreams
But this love was always so big
An encapsulating phenomenon
It was my world
And it will always be.

Seeking oneself

I was holding on,
This was my last attempt
But *He* caught my hand
A steady pull
A warm hug
I was there
In *his* glorious mercy

I scavenged the earth
Tried to find *him* in his creations
Until I found *him*.
He has sheltered me,
Fed me and nursed me.
When the world leaves you,
It is *He* who holds you.

*Allah**,
As I call upon him
In fear and happiness
But yet *he* remembers me more

Five times a day;
He is *Al- Ghaffar**
So I seek his forgiveness

Because my poem will never suffice
In delivering his excellence.

(*Allah = God in Arabic , *Al - Ghaffar = Allah's attribute for being the most forgiving)

The Tumultuous 20's.

The grief that fills my heart,
Ends up at the corners of my eyes
The trembling of my words
And my muffled cries

I think about the days gone
Each day a battle with myself
How will I ever explain anyone?
The loneliest I've ever been is with myself.

20 years,

Isn't that a long time?
So much of damage caused
Yet no one to save us.

You're trying to get better at this
This living thing
And everyone is already so ahead
It feels like you're at the starting line

If there is destiny
I won't ask about my soulmate

I just wanted to know
Is there a time when I get to just be happy?

My cat and I

Each night as I am about to sleep
A cat meows at my door
I peak through my key hole
And gently open the door

The cat curls up on my feet
Drags me with her for adventures
We stay up all night, we feel alive
Although we don't like each other

Yet I always find myself with her
Astonishing, I share my secrets with her
While she's busy planning my murder
What shall I do?

I think the cat is trying to help me
It has healed my heart
Yet it keeps trying to break it again
What shall I do?

And still each night,
Just as I am about to sleep
I once again wait for the meowing
Dear cat,

I shall meet you soon.

Life's challenges

And I know when I say it was a tough time
You think to yourself of a bad day
But I know it was a bad life

Here I am the living proof
That if things get heavy
You get the option to put them down
And when paths get blurry
You get to choose one again

But tonight I ask you too see
Who you really have been
I know you feel, the world would be better without you
And, you're going to have to wait to see it's not true.

If the wounds start coming to the surface
Caress them with care, they need some love and
patience.
Be gentle yet free;
We don't want it to be a part of our identity.
Just wait patiently,
Your time is coming too.
Until then, I'll always be here for you

Whether in a form of a poem
Or just another human.

Ambiguity of time

Sometimes, I feel like time is a thief
In my mundane life ;
it steals moments,
I want to cherish this cup of tea with mom but I can't capture it
When I was younger, there would be school, homework and coming back home.
Time is a thief. I never had enough play.
I have a personal grudge against time
If time was a person, I would cut ties
Time has taken so much away
Time makes me feel stagnant
I am angered by people who tell me they remember time well
What do you mean? I thought it just passed me by
Time is such a thief!
Time has stolen all my beautiful memories
And replaced it with the saddest ones.
Time is a thief and it keeps on stealing
I shall not forgive time for all the damage it has done!
On this stage of life the best of comedies seem to be played out by time.

Truth and lies

Lies,
Right through your white teeth
You hold your jaw wide open
While these lies escape your mouth
"I didn't do that!"
"I don't mean that"
"I'm sorry"
A mouth that lies
A mouth that eats
What a waste,
I AM BROKEN
You say
What a lie
I LOVE YOU
What a lie
A filth you keep diving in
Your own filth
Your disgusting lies
Your disgusting niceness
A manipulation
I see through it
I should have known
A dream that you are
Is a nightmare you will become

Your soft hands that embrace
Are the pointy nails that pierced
Your lips that touch
Are the teeth that bite
And the voice that sweet
Is from the devil if I might
There you are,
Pretending to be ordinary
But I see the evil within you
There is no escape
within your reach
Lies
Right through your white teeth.

Loneliness of a house

There is a scent that follows me,
In the loneliness of my house.
Sometimes, it's a loving embrace
And mostly a dreadful reality.
I think there is something lurking around
Maybe, the flowers for my future
Or the graveyard to my past?
I am not as hopeless as I used to be,
Maybe it's in these prayers I feel
Something divine seems to call me
He says " I am here"
Ah what a loving embrace.
I lingered around everywhere for this scent
And I always find it in the most;
Quiet places, intimate spaces
And lost chases.
The poet in me,
Has found poetry.

Self Identity

I am a Muslim,
Even when you don't want me to be
I am a Muslim
Even when you hate me
I am a Muslim
Even when I don't look like one
I am a Muslim
Even when its not ramzan
I am a Muslim
Even when you can't pronounce my name
I am a Muslim
Even when I don't talk like one
I am a Muslim
Even when all of my existence is being diminished by you;
Even when you want to denounce me
Even when you want to exclude me
Even when you say my homeland is not mine anymore.
I am a Muslim;
Regardless of what you think I am,
Because its us that knows
Grounded in humility,
Measured by gratitude
Brought up by values

How dare you,
Why would you?
Who told you?
Where have you learnt to bury such deep hatred for us?
Don’t you think someone taught you?
Perhaps its time to open your eyes,
Don’t let them feed you any lies
See the truth for what it is
Here is the first & last time
I write a poetry in a form of plea.

The Dark Forest

Once I lived in the forest
A dark & weary road ahead
Surrounded by animals;
Foes that look like lovers
& lovers that looked like enemies
What a tragedy it had been
A dream so scary
That I always tried to wake up
But there was no escape
Sometimes the misery is too much
The human is unable to handle it
Unless you know
This is the time to run;
& when you do, don't look back
This is your ticket to freedom
Go back to the people who love you;
There will always be someone waiting with open arms to receive you
Look,there they are
All this time never stopped loving you.
The forest is a dangerous place
But remember the lessons you learnt
It's only meant for escapes
Dreams are to be woken up from,

What about you?
Are you still dreaming?

Religion and Peace

What they don't tell you about us :
We live in small spaces but always well kept.
Smiles always crease on our faces when we eat good food
Fragrances of *attar* that linger in our houses,
A carpet in each room & curtains that match our furniture
Some mandatory *Rooh-Afza* bottles to quench your thirst when you drop by-
Some beautifully stitched **Musallah's* for when you hear the **azaan.*
Seasonal fruits & dates lying somewhere near the microwaves.
All of this along with
An undying love for oneself
& the community around us
The neighbors we love,
The acceptance we deserve
The same heart as yours
Truly human-
Things they don't tell you about us.

(* Musallah = Prayer mat, Azaan* = Call for prayer)

Love

I'm not sure, people understand?
this romanticism of love
& Demonising of it
Either I see poets writing how deeply they were hurt by love
Or an endless love dialogue on finding the charmingly perfect partner,
It's kind of devastating,
The way we are so far away from reality,
Love is not central to romance
Love is you
Love is me
& love is us
Everything else is a part of the endless
cycle we follow through our lives.
Its often "If only I find the perfect.."
Not " I wish I'm the one I love"
I think there's only so much others can help us,
It will always be our decision to change ourselves
Or change others.

Battling Fears

Before leaving,
I was so sure that it's not worth it.
I reached to the pool,
Dipped my toes to test
The temperature, you know?
Like always I expected it to be cold
And I was so scared
Because the cold water sends shivers through my spine.
Nonetheless I removed my robe and jumped in without hesitation.
To realise the water was so warm
The perfect temperature,
I was so calm now
And overjoyed as well.
The decisions we take
The risks we take
Without knowing the end result
It is indeed a great feeling
You know? To just put ourselves out there.
Despite all our possibilities of failure
We strive to live,laugh and love another day.
Life is going to the pool,
One day at a time
Isn't it?

Mystery of being Human

In the palms of my hand,
I was collecting myself
Through the sea water
Most of which seeped out
From the spaces between my fingers
Just like me,
It's seeping out
And I've been gathering myself.
Completely misunderstood that,
I was whole, there was nothing missing.
My palms are dry today,
Even though I want to dive in the sea water again,
It feels good to know, my essence couldn't be collected by anyone ;
Including myself.
The sea water calls me
And I wave goodbye
The salt is sweeter now,
And the sky is calling.

Fresh Wounds

You see these cuts on my fingers
And the blood dripping from them
I have band aided them the 3rd time today,
It still hurts, everything still hurts.
Life never changes dramatically into a fairy tale, does it?
We break ourselves only to build ourselves .
For how long do we do that? There is no scoreboard for
that.
If there is a feeling so divine to love someone
If there is a reason to be alive
If there is any sense to the being of humaneness.
Wouldn't we all rather dream then?
Dreams are the escape we all need
That's why sleep is peace.
Someday, you won't escape
And that is day the you will realise
Why is it that I still band- aid the cuts on
my fingers.

To, younger me

Between the ruins of the city,
I stand tall next to you
Tears and joy
The nature unlike anything
So peaceful yet so chaotic
You're my only building
And yet you don't realise
Just how beautiful
Everything about you is magic
My tongue has never taken a moment to stop from the everflowing- sweetness that drips with talking about you.
Beautifully, inexplicably you.
Between the ruins of the city
The most strong connection was
You and me.

The Sparrows

It's kind of crazy isn't it?
These sparrows? I used to see them so often.
I would see them from my window chirping whenever I was playing
I was just so used to them, I never paid attention.
Just like a regular background music I'd always hear
But, they disappeared didn't they?
Now that I see them, I'm surprisingly happy
Almost reminds me of how I didn't notice them when they were there.
Sometimes, we really do notice the absence of something only when it's gone isn't it?
Just like the childhood that we desperately try to outgrow
But we're all just playing adults aren't we?

The Sea and I

I had once seen you across the shore
I was about to dive in the deep sea
And that's when you held my hand.
A desperate attempt to stop me,
I was frantically moving my hand.
The waters were washing my feet
And the sand was holding me hostage.
I had to let you go,
I had to dive in.
After my long search in the blue sea
I survived all the hardships.
It was only then did I see you again at the shore.
This time, I could only see the mirror.
You no more could hold back my power,
Now I am the queen of the sea
While you're just a remain of my past.

Isolation or freedom

I'm observing, while words leave your mouth at a speed
I cannot comprehend.
Your words have depth and layers of concepts, I haven't
heard about
I look at you, almost lost and gazingly.
You dont stop, its almost like a rehearsed speech.
I can see the tension building in your bones.
You have fidgety hands
Sweaty palms and a parched throat asking for water.
You glance at me, I smile and you smile back.
Almost like a rehearsed reaction.
You are slowly easing up, and your speech is becoming
more comprehensible.
I guess that's how it works doesn't it?
Love was supposed to comfort us when we couldn't
comfort ourselves.
You've broadly advertised and made us
fantasise that only romantic relationships could do that.
But what does one do when they don't?
They hide, cover and shiver alone.
And who is to be blamed? When they don't make it out
alive on their own?
You or them?

Drums of the heart

The heart has muffled beats
Its often trying to stay alive
There is a glimmer of hope
And a sadness that fills in occasionally.

The heart has muffled beats
I've been pounding it ever since 12
It's there but doesn't call out my name anymore
It has a melancholy to its music.

The heart has muffled beats
I'm the heart
Often trying to be loud
But my screams
Often muffled with a pillow so heavy
It leaves my fingernails deeply ingrained in them.
The heart has muffled beats..

Red Indian Saree

Red pleated sari,
Hair parted with grey streaks
Her hands adjoining together as the train leaves
Her lips moving in prayers,
And her right foot resting on the empty space next to me.
Strong women know when power should be exercised
And when only prayers can help others.
They know when to let the wind through their hair.
And when to make you breathless.
The red pleated sari,
The power in her eyes.
The rage on her face
And the scream of freedom from her lungs.
I could hear it all, that day on the train
When I saw her in a red pleated sari.

Being a Woman

We are always a little too much
You can apply red lipstick but
Wipe it off, it gives the wrong impression
You can sit comfortably but
Close your legs, it gives the wrong impression
You have the right to speak but
Stop talking about feminism, it gives the wrong
impression
Keep your makeup subtle, keep your legs folded and
your mouth shut.
You are a woman after all.

Buy all the clothes you want but
Don't buy anything revealing, it gives the
wrong impression.
Do your makeup but
Keep it natural, it gives the wrong impression
Have some dreams but
Don't think you can accomplish them, it gives the wrong
impression
Get married soon but
Don't date someone, it gives the wrong impression.
Keep your skin covered, face naturally beautiful, don't

have a dream and just get married.
You are a woman after all.

Kindness

The colors of the people I see everyday,
are certainly unlike the ones you've seen.
Last Wednesday, I was rummaging through my bag to find my pen
When a strange hand offered me one "is this what you're looking for?"

3 weeks earlier I went to a cafe, I saw an hourglass.
Out of boredom I turned it upside down to pretend to time my meal, only to see a stranger smiling at me with a thumbs up sign.
Two days ago, I was riding in the taxi to college
When the driver asked me "How does the
college admission process? I'm asking since my son wanted admission"
And oh the politeness and thankfulness in his voice.

And yesterday, someone sent me a link directing me to an article about "10 traits strong women have"
They said they remembered me as soon as they read this.
Call it poetic if you want but good deeds still happen.
The world is not as black as you think it is
If we keep telling ourselves it was mere coincidence
maybe they will eventually stop existing.

For all I know is, even if today you can't find these
I hope tomorrow, the day after that and the year after
that you do.
Because you, Yes YOU deserve kindness.
And kindness is just waiting around the
corner waiting for you to acknowledge its existence.

Haunting Dreams

Last night I had a dream
It was you and I
We were together laughing
Everything was the same
The love was still there
And so was life
But I woke up
It was still dark outside
I was drenched in sweat
And none of this was real anymore
Because I was still asleep,
This was a dream inside a dream
You've gone so far away that my reality never crosses paths with you anymore
And I'm glad because some people are better as dreams.
The ones that you never wake up from and the ones that you're desperately trying to
wake up from,
Let someone be a dream.
Let someone never be your reality.

Mercy Of Death

Beep beep beep
Horizontal line.
Death? Is that you?
Knocking on my door while I'm still alive?
What do you want this time?
Willingness to live?
Or the eagerness to die?
Don't worry, I can still look you in the eye
I'm not afraid. I have never been.
You'll ask me why?
I'll tell you with sentences longer than my life.
Why this mind has made me believe in the things at the other side
Why the sunshine doesn't cross my path anymore
Why I want to go back to that one moment I felt alive.
You'll have your answer then?
But tell me, oh death!
Do you think after listening to this,
You'll not look at me with doubtful eyes?
Tell me you wont pat my head and say "But child can you hear others cries?"
Tell me now, before I tell you the stories I have tried to hide.
Tell me this moment will you try to find me even when

the blue sky turns the colour of red wine? When this heart doesn't call your name anymore, will you look for me?
Or you'll forget I ever existed and was a part of your dream?

Hope and the World

If you hear voices
That have stories that others might forget

If you rise and speak your truth
That are lies everyone has denied
If you still think the power is within you
That not only you but, others can see too

If these are the things that make you
Then maybe there is some hope for this world too.

Acceptance

No, I understand that maybe it's the strands of my hair
Maybe the curl of my lip
The moves that I do
The laughter that annoys you
The hair you want me to cut
The jokes you don't want to listen too
Maybe it the was the beginning and the very end;
The things that you once treasured are the same things that you don't blink an eye to.
It's almost as if I am like the water at the sea that you embrace only when the tears that flow are saltier than my presence.
But I am not the sea, unlike the waves I cannot return to the place I once left.
I am but the rainbow under the sun, if captured will be tainted for life.

Self Love

I thought you've known all along, yet here I am putting
it in words
I'm in love with the big brown beautiful eyes you have
the bouncy curls that fall on your shoulders,
the laughter that you spill when you see something
funny
the curves of your body
the tap of your feet
the size of your wrist
the care that you give
the tears that you've wiped
if you're thinking I'm talking about someone else, you're
wrong because all this while I've been falling in love
with myself over and over and over again
a hundered billion times, I'm in love with myself.

Maps

If you trace your fingers on the mapped roads of my
body and utter "I don't like this one"
Then know that I'll not have spaces left for you to fill in
I will leave you deserted in the middle of nothing
If you don't like me for being human
then its better you take the road that leads you out
I've never entertained nomads, never will.
because they seem to take up and adjust in a place which
is a home you built carefully with every brick
And, then suddenly leave destroying the walls and
removing the paints off them
As if the previous home was not everything they
dreamed of
And that this was just another destination to the fables
they'll recall at night.

Regrets

Deserted Love

Years from now when memories flash,
You'll realise what you had
Maybe then you will imagine how it would've been.
Or like the rain your tears will fall in between
It'll then feel like time slipping out your hands
But know that you'll be standing alone in a desert full of sand and just when you'll build up the courage to say the words; you'll understand I've faded like the oasis you thought you saw but was a mirage full of dreams.

Love and Wine

Love often ages like wine
when stored in the cellar for years, and its value only increases
just like the way you circle your finger around the rim,
tap the glass,
swirl it in an oscillatory motion,
take it so close to your lips,
yet it only reached your tongue
never out loud.
You dont have the courage
to tell the truth
but the taste, the taste of this red wine
is so addictive
and that is why you always lift your glass, and take it close to your lips.
Thats why, the wine
doesn’t leave you,
and you let it age like love
because love often ages like wine.

Finding Happiness

a cloud of feelings,
a river of words
a rain of my tears
a blurry vision
yet so much clarity ahead
what I can see from this place
the endless possibilities,
the happiness that i'll create
surrounded by the people I love
laughter playing in the background of this beautiful movie
It will be me,
standing on the cliff of the beautiful mountain
smile as wide as the sun.
I will see the days where my happiness will be the brightest.
I've seen enough dark storms.
Don't I deserve some warm and, comforting wind to hold me tight when the loneliness
creeps on me more than usual?
When the words that escape my mouth sound like pure poetry as if it were covered with multiple layers of honey.
You'll tell me to stop,

Your hand is covering my lips, but how will I ever
explain to you that I have longed for this moment.
And if it weren't for these words that I spoke, I would
not be here with you.
And you- my love? Would not be here with me.

Cold Tea

A whiff of you,
Some cold tea
Your hand wrapped around my waist
I know it faded away
Like the moisture from the air
The rainbows from my sky
The memory from my mind
A whiff of you,
Some cold tea
I'm here but you don't hold me.

Letting Go

I wear my past memories like those rugged clothes from my wardrobe.
Nobody wants to see me with it but it's the only thing that gives me comfort.
It's funny the more I wear the clothes and carry my past memories it becomes a part of my identity I cannot detach with ;
Why do we tend to hold on to things that should be forgotten?
Why is it that these old clothes that should've been given away still sit in my closet?
Is it because just like my memories I've attached a part of my soul to it?
Well, maybe today i'll let the memories be with me a bit longer
I know, holding on is toxic
I know, it's time to let go
But I also know that these are the only things I want to treasure in the corner of my heart when the darkness is growing,
this will be my only sunlight.
Until then, I won't let go.

Rented Spaces

often crowded in the spaces of my head
You tend to take a lot of place
Rented it is, yet you act like own it
Been trying to not be polite and push you out as you're not a good tenant
But something about you makes me want to let you lay your head on my lap while I run my fingers through your hair and all we are talking about is how that one time as a kid you fell down and that's how you got this mark on your head
we laugh so hard, its the best kind of laughter I've experienced.
The laughter always echoes in the empty space of my room
ever since you stopped renting.
no more are you a tenant, not even a passerby.
I only catch glimpses of you now.
As if this wasn't once where you rested for
a home when you couldn't find any.

Country and Its people

Everyone's a beggar here,
You see someone sitting on the streets
Their arms open and they say "In the name of God bestow me"
You drop money in their hands preferably the smallest denomination
You scoff, too many beggars in my country.

You are now seated in the train and you hear someone singing "The giver is him, the taker is him, give me what you can. O' traveler"
You scoff too many beggars in my country.

You reach your office and you tell your colleague
"Don't worry this time I'll definitely convince boss for a promotion"
Your friend says "You won't believe what happened! He finally called! Everything
feels great"
You both scoff too many beggars in my country.

But you never learn:
Everyone is a beggar here,
Whether for money

Or love
Whether for recognition
Or some affection
Whether a house to stay
Or some food to eat.
You are what you scoff at
You are
You are
You are.

Winters

I was a regular invite to the winters,
always there,
sitting, stirring and moping
deep exasperated breaths
tearful eyes,
a hopelessness so addictive
winter never wanted to leave,
neither did I
the cold, you'd hope would make me shiver
but the cold was a blanket of comfort
wrapped around so tightly,
yet I was breathless
and then there was summer,
knocking, shaking and thumping the door
It said it'd help me,
I refused. I said winter is home and I will not leave it
until I realized I've always been a summer child
winter has never asked me to stay
yet summer keeps calling me
that's when I decided;
winters should only be met
do not build a house out of it
enter and leave as you please
but do not stay, please don't.

Let summer warm your heart,
dance around with you, and build a house so strong,
winter will not invite you anymore.
Maybe occasionally, but never everyday.

Invisibility

I’m uncomfortable in my own space.
The air today feels toxicated
This feeling of being choked is too familiar
Surrounded by many, Recognized by none
Invisibility is something that soothed me always,
Today somehow I feel like I'm lost in the woods walking
through the darkness in the wake of the day.

Survivor

Saved,yet again while drowning
Coughing out water while fighting to breathe
They told me to go to the shallows but I always end up in the depths.
Maybe it's the heavy soul I carry around
Or merely the corpse of my past regrets
I am just hoping for a successful swim. Is that too much to ask?
I will not let the forceful waves control my breathing anymore.
I will rise to see the sun beaming once again.

Ever - flowing Time

5,6,7,8
I count on my fingers
Its been 8 mins since you left
but yet it feels like you left an eternity ago
your last hug, the way you held me
did not feel real anymore
there is seldom a point where I knew
you knew, but we weren't ready yet
I guess we can never be ready
whether the beginning or the ending
In love there is no definite start or end
Its either butterflies or hollows
you don't count love by days, weeks or seasons
Its there in a minute and not in the other
5,6,7,8 I count on my fingers,
Its been 8 months since I first fell in love with you.
yet it feels like an eternity.

www.ingramcontent.com/pod-product-compliance
Lightning Source LLC
Chambersburg PA
CBHW070646240926
51846CB00003BA/796
9789370923744